THE WHITE HOUSE

1600 Pennsylvania Avenue

THE
WHITE
HOUSE

1600 Pennsylvania Avenue

The White House has been the official home for all presidents of the United States of America except for George Washington, the first president.

BY JON WILSON

GRAPHIC DESIGN
Robert A. Honey, Seattle

PHOTO RESEARCH
James R. Rothaus, James R. Rothaus & Associates

ELECTRONIC PRE-PRESS PRODUCTION
Robert E. Bonaker, Graphic Design & Consulting Co.

Library of Congress Cataloging-in-Publication Data
Wilson, Jon
The White House : 1600 Pennsylvania Avenue / by Jon Wilson
p. cm.
Summary: Traces the historical development of the home of the
presidents of the United States, describing how the mansion
has grown from six rooms in 1798 to 132 rooms today.
ISBN 1-56766-544-6 (library bound : alk. paper)

1. White House (Washington D.C.) — Juvenile literature.
2. Washington (D.C.)—Buildings, structures, etc.—Juvenile literature.
3. Presidents—United States—History—Juvenile literature.
[1. White House (Washington D.C.) 2. Presidents—History] I. Title

F204.W5W718 1998   98-26998
975.3 — dc21   CIP
                                                                AC

CONTENTS

A New Nation 7

Finding a Capital 8

Designing a Palace 11

Work Must Go On 12

Attack on the Palace 15

200 Years 16

Big Family, Bigger House 19

The Tour 20

America's Address 23

Index & Glossary 24

A NEW NATION

Before the United States became a nation, its 13 colonies were ruled by the King of England. In 1776, the people of America decided that it was time to stand on their own. They announced their freedom from British rule by writing the *Declaration of Independence*. Then they fought for their freedom in the *War of Independence*. Finally, after eight years and many battles, the Americans won the war, and the United States of America was born. Americans had worked hard and given their lives to see this dream of freedom come true—but the work was just beginning.

This portrait of George Washington was painted by James Peale in the 1760s, about 15 years before he became the first president of the United States of America.

The new nation needed a leader, and it needed laws and rules. Political and military leaders from throughout the country met to decide these important subjects at a *Constitutional Convention*. During the meeting, *General George Washington*, a hero of the War of Independence, was elected as the nation's first president. The *Constitution*, the document that described how the new government would work, was also created.

FINDING A CAPITAL

Another difficult question needed an answer: What city would be the new nation's **capital**? A capital is the city where the nation's government is officially based. There was much discussion over choosing the new capital of the United States. New York and *Philadelphia* were at the top of the list. Philadelphia had already been the temporary capital from 1790 to 1800. But President George Washington had another idea. He suggested that the capital should not be a part of any one state. Instead, it should be a new city.

A swampy piece of land along the *Potomac River* was chosen for the new capital. It would be the site of the *Presidential Palace* and the center of government. The marshy land needed to be drained before any building could take place. The new city would be called *Washington, District of Columbia*, to honor the nation's first president as well as explorer Christopher Columbus.

In 1794 Andrew Ellicott made this print. It shows the planned sites for the Capitol and White House. Pierre L'Enfant designed the original street plans three years earlier.

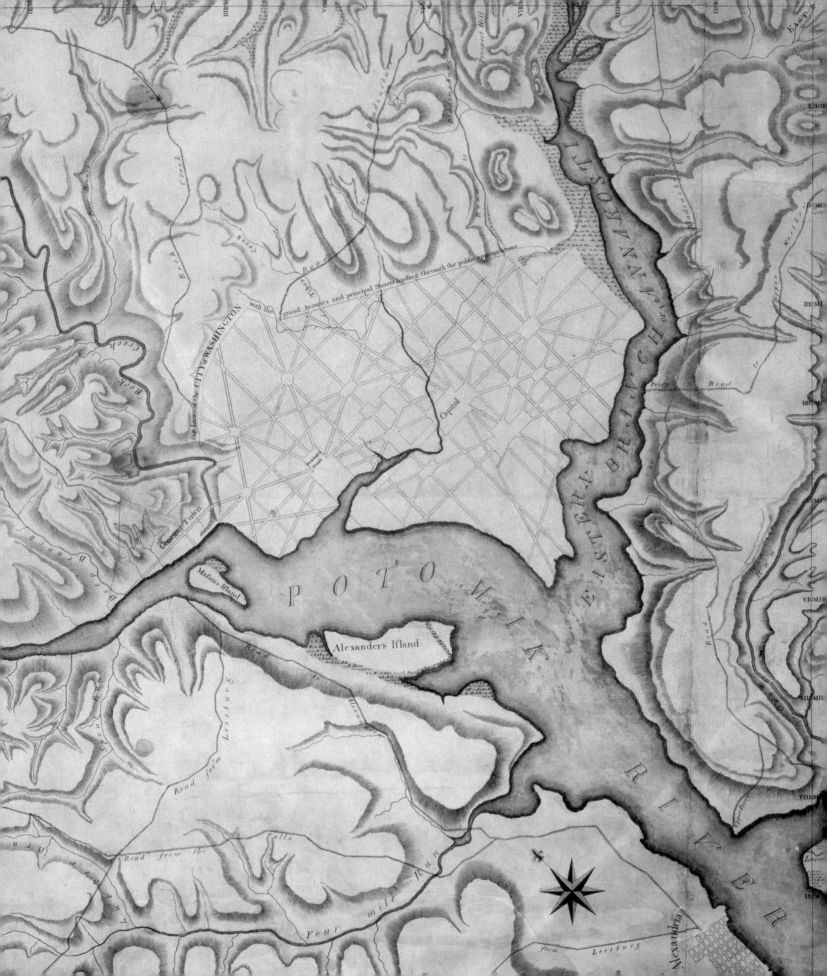

SCALE 10 FEET TO AN INCH

NORTH ELEVATION

EXECUTIVE MANSION
DRAWN FROM ARRANGEMENTS
OFFICE AIRED

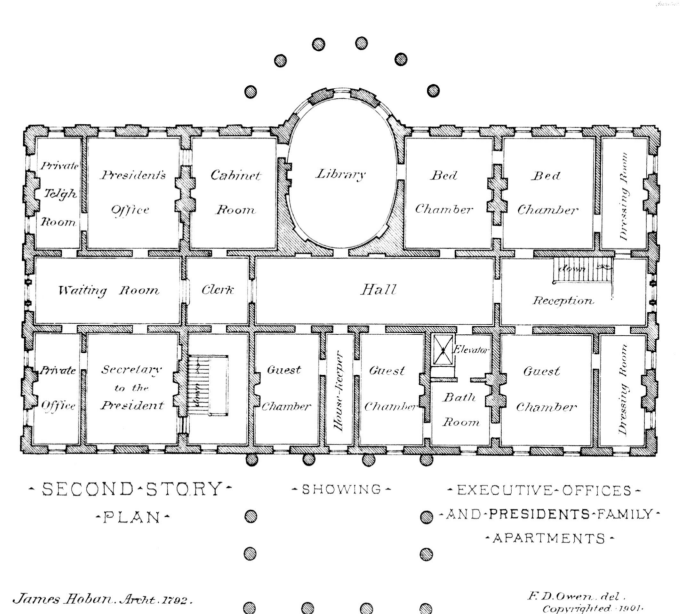

| Private Telgh Room | President's Office | Cabinet Room | Library | Bed Chamber | Bed Chamber | Dressing Room |

Waiting Room | Clerk | Hall | | | Reception | *down*

| Private Office | Secretary to the President | | Guest Chamber | House-keeper | Guest Chamber | Bath Room *Elevator* | Guest Chamber | Dressing Room |

·SECOND·STORY·   ·SHOWING·   ·EXECUTIVE·OFFICES·
·PLAN·   ·AND·PRESIDENTS·FAMILY·
                                       ·APARTMENTS·

James Hoban. Archt. 1792.

F. D. Owen. del.
Copyrighted 1901.

DESIGNING A PALACE

Top:
This drawing of the White House was created in 1853 by Thomas U. Walter.

Bottom:
F. D. Owen in 1901 made this floor plan of the second story in the White House. It was originally designed by James Hoban in 1792.

While the swamp was being drained, a contest was held to decide what the Presidential Palace would look like. Many people entered the contest, including Thomas Jefferson, who wrote the Declaration of Independence. The winning plan was by an **architect**, or building designer, named *James Hoban*. Hoban designed a long, boxlike building with a triangular roof held up by large columns.

Work on the Presidential Palace began in 1792. Bricks were made at the construction site. White sandstone was brought in from stone quarries in the state of Virginia. The finest **stonemasons**, experts at building with stone, were hired in Scotland and brought to America. Lumber from the states of North Carolina and Virginia was also used for the construction. The best carpenters from all across the nation began working on the home of America's president.

While the Presidential Palace was being built, President Washington conducted business at offices in Philadelphia and his home in Mount Vernon. Important leaders from around the world came to Washington's home. Martha Washington and her two daughters helped entertain the guests. George Washington helped lay the palace's **cornerstone**—the ceremonial first stone for the new building. He also oversaw the construction, but his time as president ended before the building was finished.

George Washington's home in Mount Vernon, Virginia. This photograph was taken in 1997.

In 1796, *John Adams*, one of the signers of the Declaration of Independence, was elected as the nation's second president. Like George Washington, President Adams conducted government business in the temporary offices in Philadelphia. During his last year as president, Adams was able to move into the Presidential Palace. Only six rooms were completed, and there were many unfinished walls and staircases. However, the president and the nation finally had a home.

ATTACK ON THE PALACE

The British soldiers, and the burning of the Presidential Palace, are shown in this drawing which was created to record the events of August 14, 1814.

In 1812 the United States went to war with England once again. *James Madison* was the president during this difficult time. On August 14th, 1814, British soldiers sailed up the Potomac River and attacked Washington, D.C. President Madison and his wife Dolly barely escaped capture. They took with them many important papers and a painting of George Washington. The British soldiers set the Presidential Palace on fire. A summer thunderstorm helped put the fire out, but much of the building's white sand-stone was badly scorched.

Over the past 200 years, many things have changed at the Presidential Palace. Heating, plumbing, and a cooking stove were added in 1850. Before that, the presidents' meals were cooked in giant fireplaces. Electricity was added while *Benjamin Harrison* was President (1889–1893). Mrs. Harrison refused to turn on the lights because she was afraid the newfangled electricity would give her a shock. The building's name changed over time, too. First known as the Presidential Palace, it became the *Executive Mansion*, and finally the White House. President *Theodore Roosevelt* officially gave it the White House name.

Taken in the 1890s, this photograph shows the layout of the White House kitchen. Also seen, is one of the White House cooks.

BIG FAMILY, BIGGER HOUSE

Theodore Roosevelt with his wife Edith, daughters Alice and Ethel, and sons Theodore, Jr., Kermit, Archibald, and Quentin.

Theodore Roosevelt, his wife, and their six children moved into the White House in 1901. The large size of his family helped Roosevelt decide to add a new West Wing. The building has been remodeled many times. In the 1860s, President *Ulysses S. Grant* had the entire inside redone because of rotting timbers and a falling ceiling. The inside was redone again during *Harry S. Truman's* presidency (1948–1952), when the walls were strengthened with steel and concrete. Since 1798, the building has grown from 6 rooms to 132. It now has swimming pools, bowling alleys, and movie theaters as well as offices, bedrooms, kitchens, meeting rooms, and dining rooms.

THE TOUR

Today, about 2 million people a year visit the White House. They line up at the East Visitor's Entrance to tour the first floor, also known as the State Floor. The building is 170 feet long and 85 feet wide. The East Wing contains the office of the president's wife, who is often called the **First Lady**, and her staff. The first floor also holds the kitchen, the library, the offices of the medical staff, and the Diplomatic Reception Room. The West Wing holds the president's office, called the **Oval Office,** and other offices for his assistants. The President and his family live on the second floor. Two well-known rooms on the second floor are the Lincoln Bedroom and the Rose Guest Room.

Besides regular tours. the White House is used to entertain guests of the president. This photograph, taken in 1963, shows guests of President John F. Kennedy dancing in the East Room.

20

Tourists gather outside the White House not only to view its beauty, but with the hope of seeing either the president and his family or someone else of importance.

The White House stands in the middle of 18 beautifully landscaped acres. Since it was first occupied almost 200 years ago, it has been the site of important national and world events. It has been visited by kings and queens, diplomats, religious leaders, and politicians. It has been at the center of peace and war. Its address—1600 Pennsylvania Avenue, Washington, D.C.—is the address for the president, and for America.

GLOSSARY

architect (ARK-ih-tekt)
An architect is someone who designs and plans what a building will look like. The architect who designed the nation's Presidential Palace was James Hoban.

capital (KAP-ih-tull)
A capital is the official seat of a nation's government—the place where the government meets and makes its decisions. The capital of the United States is Washington, D.C.

cornerstone (KORN-er-stone)
A cornerstone is a stone that celebrates the official beginning of a new building project. Usually the stone is at one corner of the building, and it often has a date or other writing on it.

First Lady (FIRST LAY-dee)
The President's wife is often called the First Lady. The First Lady and her staff have offices in the East Wing of the White House.

Oval Office (OH-vull OFF-iss)
The president's office is known as the Oval Office. It is in the West Wing of the White House.

stonemason (STONE-may-sun)
A stonemason is a person who shapes stone and uses it to make walls and buildings. Stonemasons from Scotland helped build the White House.

INDEX

Adams, John, 12
architect, 11
Capital, 8, 9
Constitution, 7
Constitutional Convention, 7
cornerstone, 12
Declaration of Independence, 7, 11, 12
Executive Mansion, 16
First Lady, 20
Grant, Ulysses S., 19
Harrison, Benjamin, 16
Hoban, James, 10, 11
Madison, James, 15
Mount Vernon, 13
Oval Office, 20
Philadelphia, 8, 12
Potomac River, 8, 9, 15
Presidential Palace, 8, 11, 12, 14, 15, 16
Roosevelt, Theodore, 16, 18, 19
stonemason, 11
Truman, Harry S., 19
War of Independence, 7
Washington, D.C., 8, 9, 15, 23
Washington, George, 3, 6, 7, 8, 12, 13, 15
White House, 2, 9, 10, 16, 17, 21, 22